Viola Online String Sampler

Viola Sheet Music

By Robin Kay Deverich

Global Music School String Publications

Graphic Design by Julia Kay

ISBN 9780982385609

Copyright © 2008 Robin Kay Deverich. All Rights Reserved.

*No part of this publication may be reproduced in any form
or by any means without the prior written permission of the author.*

http://www.violaonline.com

TABLE OF CONTENTS

MEDIEVAL & RENAISSANCE PERIODS   COMPOSERS

Columba aspexit	Hildegard of Bingen	8
Sixth Royal Estampie from Chansonnier du Roy	Anonymous	9
Helas Madame	King Henry 8th	10
Kemp's Jigg	Anonymous	11
Fantasia	Thomas Lupo	12
Minuet from The Fiddle New Model'd	Robert Crome	13

BAROQUE PERIOD

Rondeau from Abdelazar	Henry Purcell	18
Hornpipe from Water Music Suite	George Frideric Handel	19
La Folia medley	Marin Marais, Arcangelo Corelli, Antonio Vivaldi	20
Double Violin Concerto in A Minor, Op. 3, No. 8, 1st movement	Antonio Vivaldi	22
Prelude from Cello Suite I in G Major	J.S. Bach	24
Allegro from Brandenburg Concerto No. 5	J.S. Bach	26
Kyrie from Messa a 4 con violini	Maurizio Cazzati	28
Medley: *He Shall Feed His Flock Like a Shepherd* and *Hallelujah Chorus* from Messiah	George Frideric Handel	30
Arioso from Cantata No. 156	J.S. Bach	32

CLASSICAL PERIOD

Ave Verum Corpus, K. 618	Wolfgang Amadeus Mozart	33
Adagio from Violin Concerto No. 3 in G	Wolfgang Amadeus Mozart	34
Andante from String Quartet No. 13 in Am	Franz Schubert	36
Andante from Emperor Quartet in C major	Franz Joseph Haydn	37
Surprise Symphony No. 94, 2nd movement	Franz Joseph Haydn	38
Pastoral Symphony No. 6, 1st and 5th movements	Ludwig van Beethoven	39

ROMANTIC PERIOD

Hungarian Dance No. 5	Johannes Brahms	40
The Moldau from Ma Vlast.	Bedrich Smetana	41
Halling from 25 Norwegian Folksongs and Dances	Edward Grieg	42
Emperor Waltz	Johann Strauss II	43
Vieille Chanson	Pauline Viardot	44
Andante from Violin Concerto in E Minor	Felix Mendelssohn	46
Allegro and *Adagio* from B minor Cello Concerto	Antonin Dvorak	47
Nocturne from String Quartet No. 2 in D major	Alexander Borodin	48
Elégie Op. 44 for Viola and Piano	Alexander Glazunov	49
Barcarolla from Sonata in Bb for Viola and Piano	Henri Vieuxtemps	50
Ave Maria from a theme by J.S. Bach	Charles Gounod/J.S. Bach	51
Sicilienne Op. 78 for cello and piano	Gabriel Fauré	52
Meditation from Thaïs	Jules Massenet	54
Habanera from Carmen	Georges Bizet	56
Reed Flutes from The Nutcracker Suite	Pyotr Ilyich Tchaikovsky	57

20th CENTURY

Overture from Pulcinella Ballet	Igor Stravinsky	58
Moderato from Sonata No. 1 in G Major	Domenico Gallo	60
Assez vif from String Quartet in F Major	Maurice Ravel	62
Sehr langsam from 4 Pieces, Op. 7	Anton Webern	63
Simple Gifts melody	Joseph Brackett Jr.	64
Braul from Romanian Folk Dances	Bela Bartok	65

NON-TRADITIONAL

The Basso	Gypsy Traditional	66
Odessa Bulgarish	Klezmer Traditional	67
Varys Hasapikos	Greek Traditional	68
El Jarabe Tapatio	Mexican Traditional	69
Jasmine Flower	Chinese Traditional	70
Sara Sara	Tyāgarāja (Carnatic)	71
Longa Nahawand	Tanburi Cemil Bey (Arabic/Ottoman)	72
Fiddle Medley	Fiddle Traditional	73
Fiddle Medley - simplified	Fiddle Traditional	74
Irish Washerwoman	Irish Traditional	75
The Ragtime Violin	Irving Berlin	76
The Castle Walk	James Reese Europe & Ford T. Dabney	77
St. Louis Blues	W. C. Handy	79

Preface

Viola Online String Sampler Viola Sheet Music is a fun and easy way to actively learn, study and play beautiful viola music from a wide variety of styles and eras. 54 pieces are featured, representing music history periods, styles and cultures, including Medieval, Renaissance, Baroque, Classical, Romantic, 20th Century, Fiddle, Klezmer, Gypsy, Chinese, Greek, Carnatic, Arabic, Mariachi, Ragtime and Blues. These arrangements have been simplified for advanced beginners to intermediate players, and provide a representative sampling of most major forms of string music such as concertos, symphonies, sonatas, quartets and trios. A study guide, sold separately, explains the history and musical form of the selected pieces, and includes viola technique tips for each piece of music.

As an added bonus, sound files of each piece are currently available on a website,* Viola Online™: *http://www.violaonline.com* In addition to sound files, Viola Online™ content includes a review of viola basics such as instrument care and tuning; viola playing position; fingering assistance; viola technique tips; scales and etudes; and music theory basics.

Making music can bring you joy, and this string sampler is designed to help you actively learn, study and play beautiful string music from a wide variety of styles and eras. Let the music begin!

No guarantees are made that these sound files and website will be available indefinitely.

Columba aspexit

Hildegard

Sixth Royal Estampie

Anonymous

Helas madame

Henry VIII

Kemp's Jigg

Anonymous

©2008 RK Deverich

Fantasia

Lupo

©2008 RK Deverich

Minuet & Finger Pattern 1

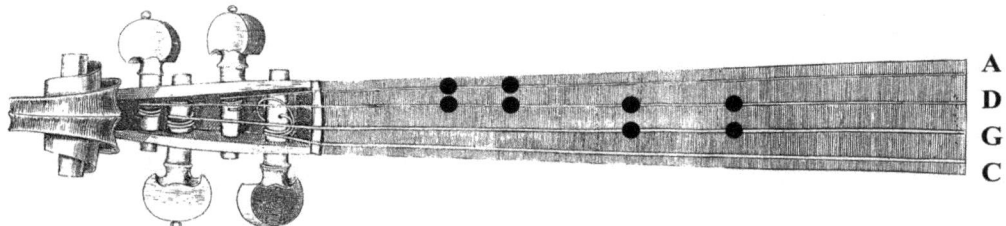

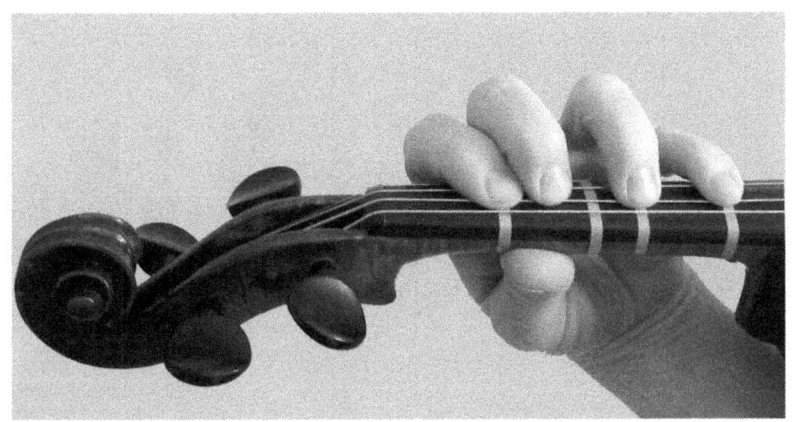

Finger Pattern 1

C Major Scale

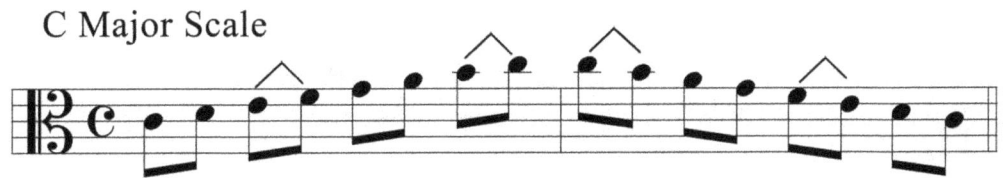

The symbol ∧ or ∨ indicates that these fingers should be placed closely together

Minuet 1

Crome

©2008 RK Deverich

Minuet & Finger Pattern 2

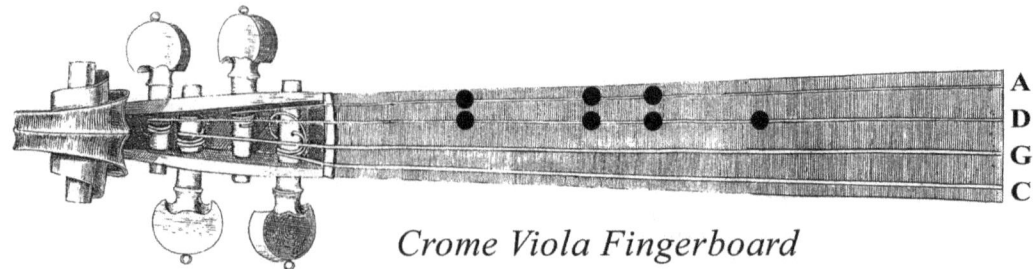

Crome Viola Fingerboard

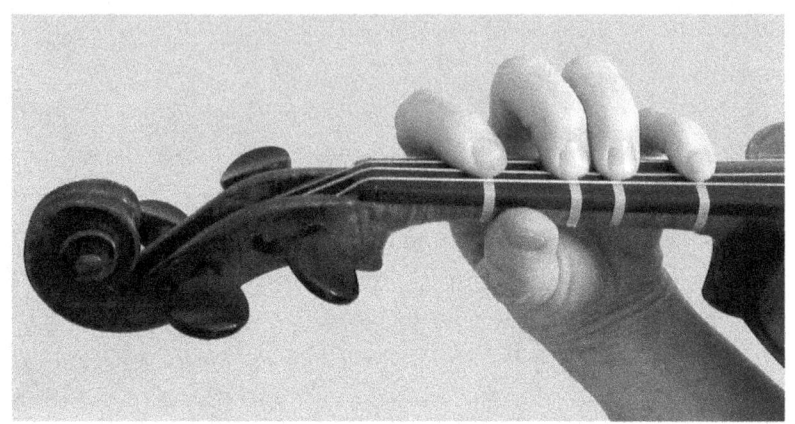

Finger Pattern 2

D Major Scale

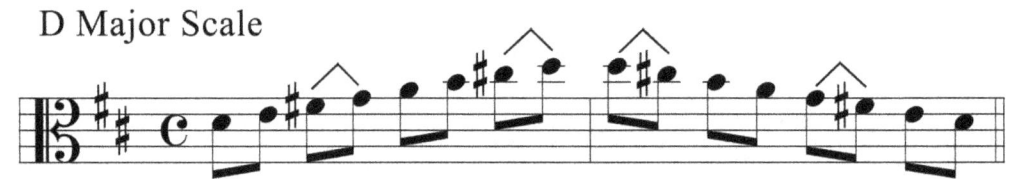

The symbol ∧ or ∨ indicates that these fingers should be placed closely together

Minuet

Crome

©2008 RK Deverich

Minuet & Finger Pattern 3

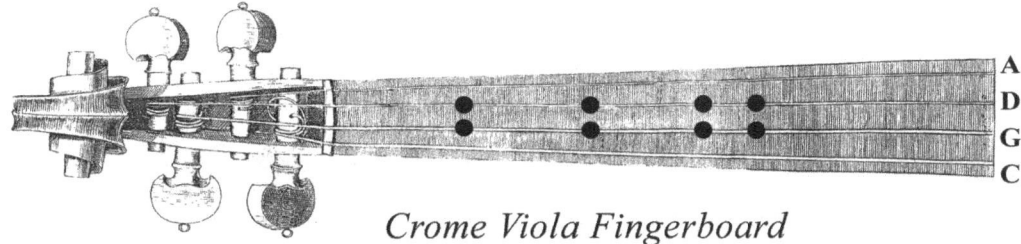

Crome Viola Fingerboard

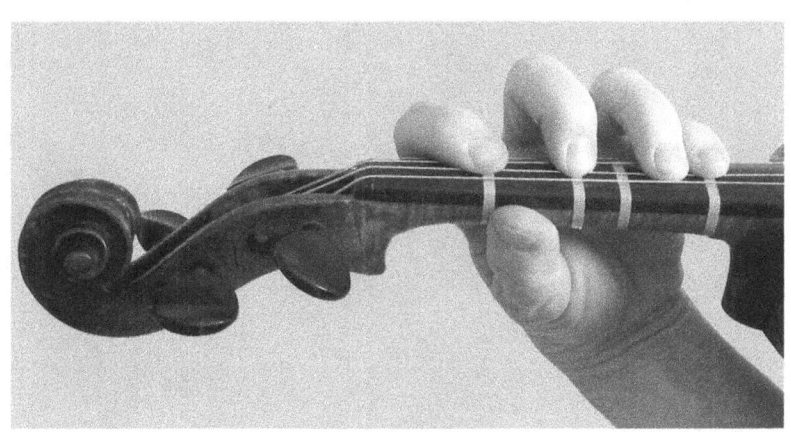

Finger Pattern 3

A Major Scale

The symbol ∧ or ∨ indicates that these fingers should be placed closely together

Minuet 3

Crome

Minuet & Finger Pattern 4

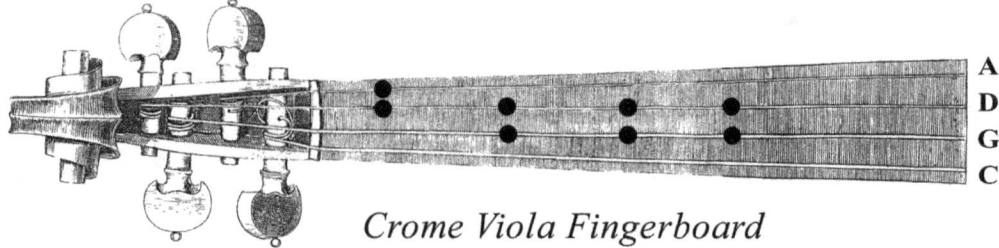

Crome Viola Fingerboard

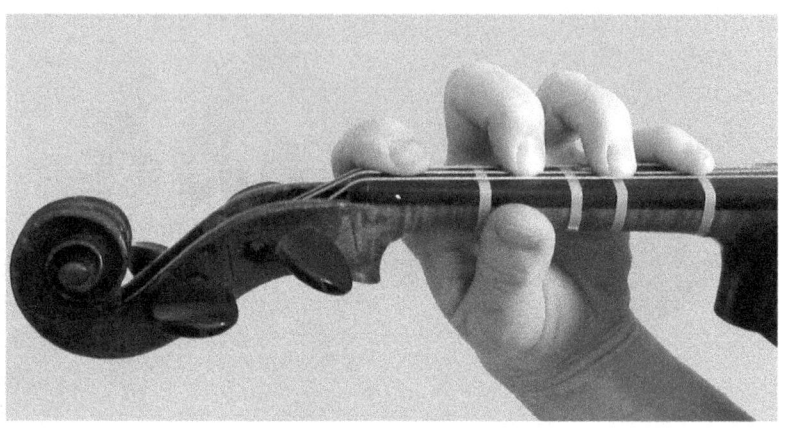

Finger Pattern 4

Bb Major Scale

Minuet 4

Crome

Minuet & Finger Pattern 5

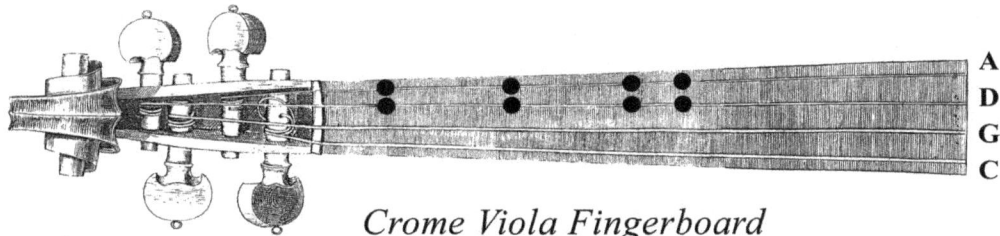

Crome Viola Fingerboard

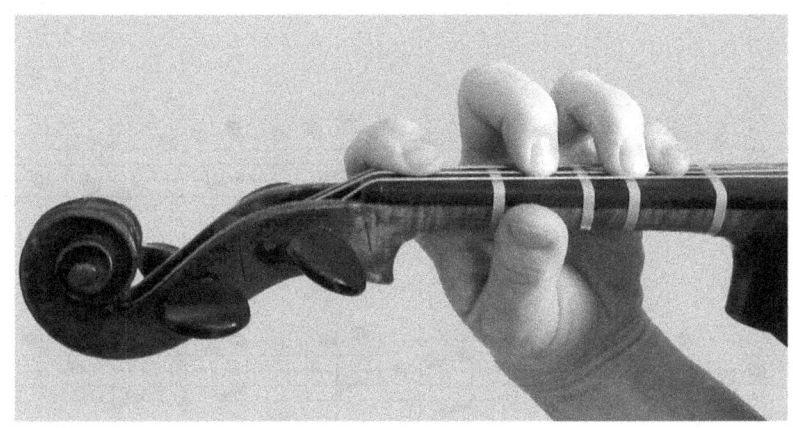

Finger Pattern 5

The symbol ∧ or ∨ indicates that these fingers should be placed closely together

Minuet 5

Crome

©2008 RK Deverich

Rondeau

Purcell

Hornpipe
from Water Music Suite in D

Handel

La Folia

Violin Concerto in A minor
1st Movement

Vivaldi

Allegro
from Brandenburg Concerto No. 5

Bach

Kyrie

Cazzati

Messiah

He Shall Feed His Flock

Handel

Arioso

Bach

Ave Verum Corpus

Mozart

Adagio
from Violin Concerto No. 3

Mozart

Andante
from String Quartet No. 13 in A minor

Schubert

Andante
from the Emperor Quartet

Haydn

Surprise Symphony

Haydn

Pastoral Symphony No. 6

Beethoven

Allegro *The awakening of joyful feelings upon arriving in the country*

Hungarian Dance No. 5

Brahms

The Moldau

from Má vlast

Smetana

Halling

Grieg

Emperor Waltz

Strauss

Vieille Chanson

Viardot

Andante
from Violin Concerto Op. 64

Mendelssohn

Cello Concerto in B Minor

Dvorák

Nocturne
from String Quartet No. 2

Andante *cantabile ed espressivo*

Borodin

Elégie

Glazunov

Barcarolla

Vieuxtemps

Ave Maria

Andante semplice

Bach-Gounod

Sicilienne

Fauré

Habanera

Bizet

Dance of the Reed Flutes
from The Nutcracker Suite

Tchaikovsky

Overture
from Pulcinella

Stravinsky

Trio Sonata No. 1
(originally attributed to Pergolesi)

Moderato

Gallo

Assez vif
from Quartet in F

Ravel

Sehr langsam
from 4 Pieces, Op. 7

Webern

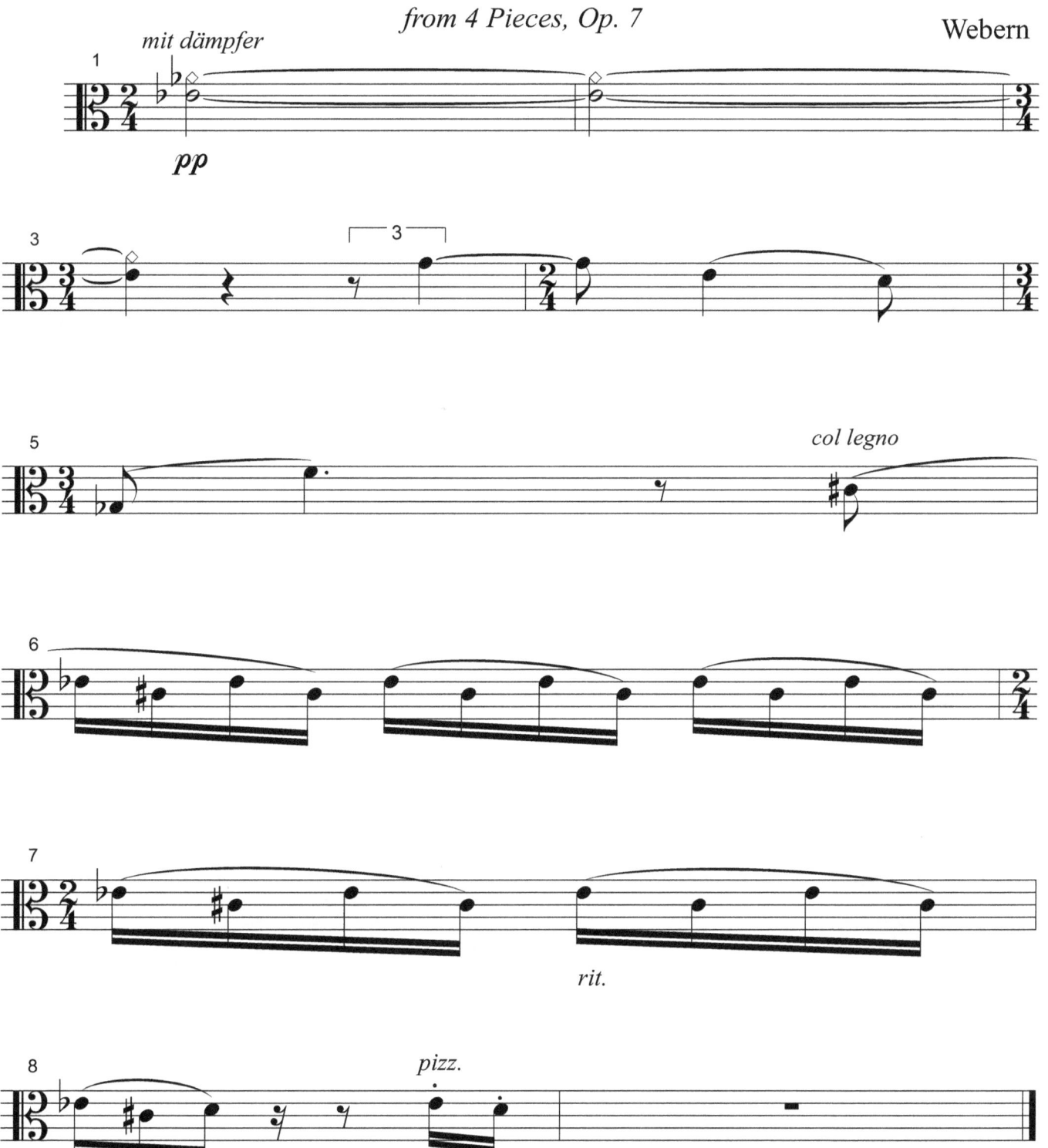

Simple Gifts

Brackett

©2008 RK Deverich

Braul

Allegro

Bartok

The Basso

Gypsy Traditional

Odessa Bulgarish

Klezmer Traditional

Varys Hasapikos

Greek Traditional

El jarabe tapatío

Mexican Traditional

Jasmine Flower

Chinese Traditional

Sara Sara

Tyagaraja

Longa Nahawand

Bey

Fiddle Medley

Fiddle Medley
(simplified)

Irish Washerwoman

Irish Traditional

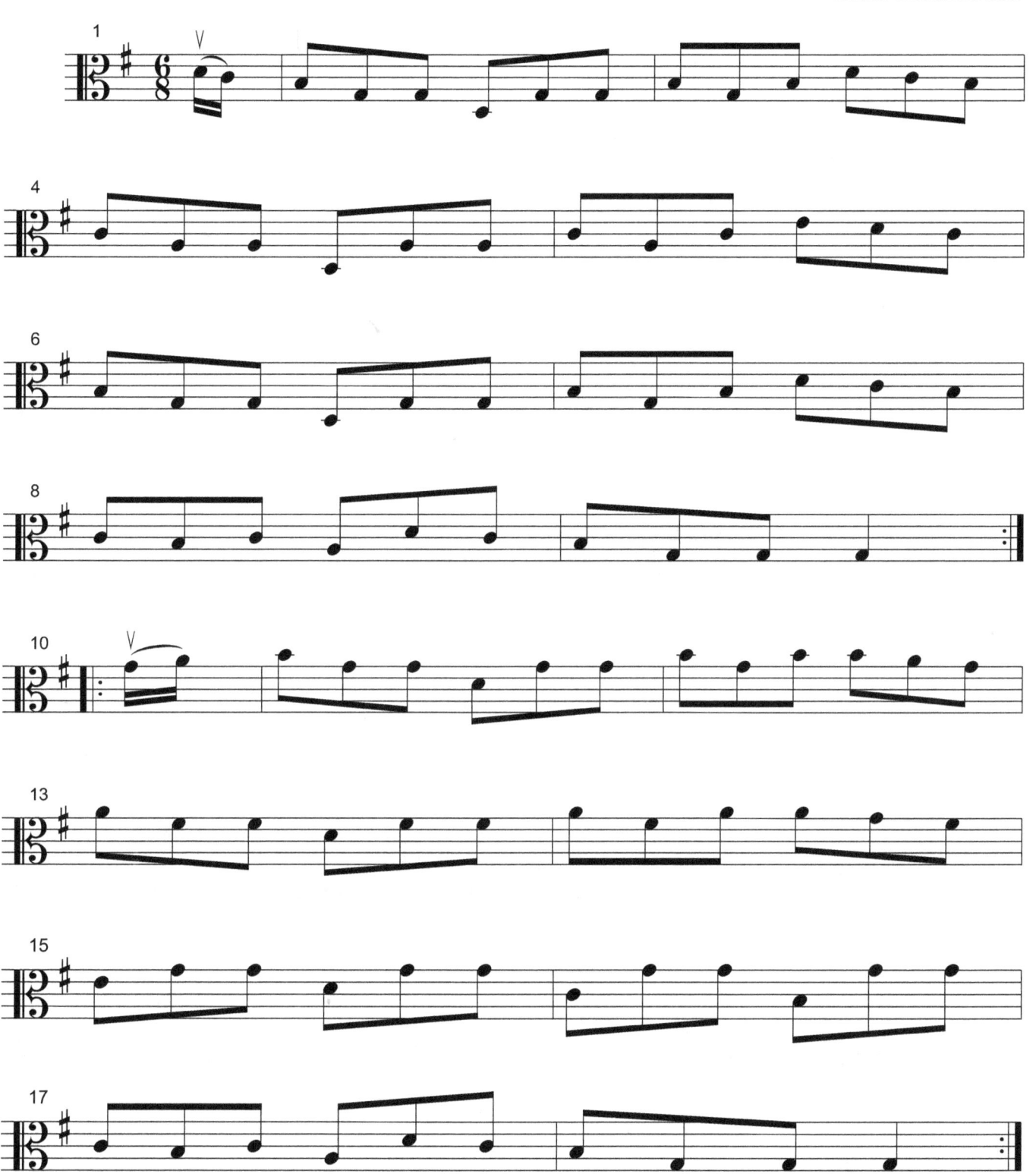

©2008 RK Deverich

Ragtime Violin

Berlin

The Castle Walk

Con spirito

Europe & Dabney

©2008 RK Deverich

St. Louis Blues

Handy

www.ingramcontent.com/pod-product-compliance
Lightning Source LLC
Chambersburg PA
CBHW081501040426
42446CB00016B/3337